# AWESOME ATHLETES

# TARA LIPINSKI

Jill C. Wheeler
ABDO & Daughters

## visit us at
## www.abdopub.com

Published by Abdo & Daughters, 4940 Viking Drive, Suite 622, Edina, Minnesota 55435.
Copyright © 1998 by Abdo Consulting Group, Inc., Pentagon Tower, P.O. Box 36036, Minneapolis, Minnesota 55435 USA. International copyrights reserved in all countries. No part of this book may be reproduced in any form without written permission from the publisher.

Printed in the United States.

Cover and Interior Photo credits: Duomo
                        Sports Illustrated


Edited by Kal Gronvall

### Library of Congress Cataloging-in-Publication Data

Wheeler, Jill C., 1964-
        Tara Lipinski / Jill C. Wheeler.
        p.  cm. -- (Awesome athletes)
        Summary: A brief biography of the youngest skater ever to win United States and World Figure Skating Championships.
        Includes Index.
        ISBN 1-56239-846-6
        1. Lipinski, Tara, 1982-  --Juvenile literature.  2. Skaters-United States--Biography--Juvenile literature.   3. Women skaters--United States--Biography--Juvenile literature. [1. Lipinski, Tara, 1982-  2. Ice skaters. 3. Women--Biography.]  I. Title. II. Series.
        GV850.L56W54     1998
        796.91' 2 092
        [B]--dc21  85685                                97-27014
                                                        CIP
                                                        AC

# Contents

A National Champion...................................... 4

Quick Learner ......................................... 6

Climbing to the Top ................................. 8

Skating Around The World ...................... 11

Inspiring Other Kids ............................. 17

Cool Under Pressure............................... 19

On To New York...................................... 22

Youngest World Champion ...................... 24

Looking Toward The Olympics ................ 27

Glossary ................................................. 30

Index ..................................................... 32

# A National Champion

It was February 15, 1997, the final night of the U.S. National Women's Figure Skating Championships in Nashville, Tennessee. Sixteen thousand spectators watched eagerly as the last competitor of the evening stepped out onto the ice. Fourteen-year-old Tara Lipinski entered the free skating final competition in second place. The pressure was on. She knew she could win—if she didn't make any mistakes.

The music began, the soundtracks from two movies–*Sense and Sensibility* and *Much Ado About Nothing.* The audience watched in amazement as the 75 pound skater flashed across the ice with grace and artistic flair. She completed each technical element of her program without the slightest error.

She also did something no other female skater had ever done before. Among her seven flawless triple jumps was a **triple loop**-triple loop combination. No female skater ever had been able to complete two triple jumps in a row before Tara. The night before, during the Ladies Short Program, she had landed a triple **lutz**-double loop combination and a triple flip. Her jumps were by far the toughest that any skater had ever tried before.

Tara's daring jumps and skill had paid off. She had become the youngest woman ever to win the U.S. National Championship.

**Tara Lipinski performing a triple jump during the Short Program.**

# Quick Learner

Tara Lipinski was born June 10, 1982, in Philadelphia, Pennsylvania. Her mother, Patricia, and father, Jack, had been high school sweethearts. The two had married after Jack finished college. Jack began a career in the petroleum industry. Eventually the family moved to Sugarland, Texas. Tara is their only child.

Tara's love affair with skating began when she was just three years old. One day someone put a pair of roller skates on her little feet. Tara loved it. She quickly became a whiz on roller skates. By the time she was only five years old she was already playing roller hockey with older boys.

When she was six years old, Tara tried on ice skates for the first time. Her parents still remember what happened.

"She was flopping around all over the place," her father recalled. "We said, 'Well, she'll never be an ice skater.' Then, Pat and I went inside for some hot chocolate. By the time we came back out, Tara was doing exactly the same things on ice she could do on roller skates."

**Quick learner, Tara Lipinski started ice skating at age 6.**

# Climbing to the Top

It was soon clear that Tara had unusual talent on the ice. Her family decided to find her a coach who could help her achieve her full potential. They interviewed and **auditioned** four famous coaches. Finally, they selected Richard Callaghan. Callaghan had worked with two other famous skaters—Todd Eldredge and Nicole Bobek.

In 1991, Tara and her mother moved to an apartment in Bloomfield Hills, Michigan, so Tara could study with Callaghan. She also joined the Detroit Skating Club.

Meanwhile, Jack stayed at the family home in Texas. He is a vice president at his company there. The family and their five dogs get together on weekends via cross-country flights. They also talk on the phone each day, and Tara's parents often travel with her to her skating competitions.

The move to Michigan paid off. In 1994, just five years after she first tried on ice skates, Tara was the national novice silver medalist. That summer, she became the youngest gold medalist in the history of the U.S. Olympic Festival.

The United States Figure Skating Association makes figure skaters pass a series of tests to move up to higher levels. There are three basic levels in figure skating, the Novice Level, the Junior Level, and the Senior Level. Skaters begin as Novices. Then they become Juniors, and finally Seniors.

Tara quickly progressed to the Junior Level. She captured first place honors at the Blue Sword competition in Germany in 1994. In 1995, she was a silver medalist at the U.S. National Junior Figure Skating Championships in Anchorage, Alaska. She was also the fourth ranked Junior that same year in the World Junior Figure Skating Championships in Budapest, Hungary.

By 1996, Tara had qualified to compete at the Senior Level. She captured a bronze medal at her first U.S. National Figure Skating Championships in San Jose, California, in 1996. The win made her one of the youngest medalists ever at that event and qualified her to go to the World Figure Skating Championships.

Tara flew to Edmonton, Alberta, to skate with the best women in the world. She finished 15th at her first World Championships competition. Tara was just getting started.

**Tara Lipinski has climbed to the top of the skating world faster than most others.**

# Skating Around The World

Tara is a lot like any teenager. She loves to spend time with her friends, especially at the shopping mall. She loves to go to movies, especially those starring Tom Cruise. She also likes to watch TV now and then, and she's wild about cooking.

Yet few teenagers have been to as many places around the world as Tara. In 1996, she competed in the Champions International Skating Series. Her first stop was in Ontario, Canada, where she placed second at Skate Canada. Just five days later, she skated to a third-place finish in Paris, France, at the Trophy Lalique.

The final stop was at the Nation's Cup in Germany. United States skating officials asked Tara to compete there in place of fellow U.S. skater Nicole Bobek, who was injured. Tara ended up taking the silver medal. She was just fractions of a point behind the gold medal winner, Russian skater Irina Slutskaya.

Throughout the Champions Series, Tara was the youngest skater on the winner's platform. That didn't matter to her. "To go from the U.S. to Canada to Paris to Germany in three weeks, and to be asked to compete against the world's best, was a little bit overwhelming," Tara said. "But once I was on the ice, I knew I was prepared. . . . I just had to perform. . . . I love the thrill of competing."

Tara rounded out her accomplishments in 1996 with a first place team finish at the U.S. Postal Service Challenge in Philadelphia, the city where she was born. It was here she first stunned audiences with her **triple loop**-triple loop combination. That feat made her the first woman in U.S. history to successfully perform that combination in competition.

**Opposite page: Tara at the
1996 USPS Challenge.**

# THE MAKING OF AN AWESOME ATHLETE

**Tara Lipinski is one of the youngest champions in skating.**

## 1982

Born June 10, in Philadelphia

## 1994

First place, U.S. Olympic Festival
First Place, Blue Swords

## 1995

Fourth place, World Junior Championships
Second place, National Junior Championships

## 1996

First place (team), U.S. Postal Service Challenge

## How Awesome Is She?

Here is how Tara Lipinski compares to some other Figure Skating Champions.

| Skater | Achievements |
|---|---|
| Peggy Fleming | Five time U.S. National Champion; Olympic Gold Medal. |
| Dorothy Hamill | Three time U.S. National Champion; Olympic Gold Medal. |
| **Tara Lipinski** | U.S. National Champion; World Champion, age 15. |
| Kristi Yamaguchi | Four time U.S. National Champ. |

# TARA LIPINSKI

**AGE: 15**
**HEIGHT: 4 Feet 8 Inches**
**WEIGHT: 75 pounds**
**HOME CLUB: DETROIT**
**SKATING CLUB**

| 1996 | 1996 | 1997 | 1997 |
|---|---|---|---|
| Second place, Nations Cup | Second place, Skate Canada | First Place, World Championships | First place, U.S. National Championships |

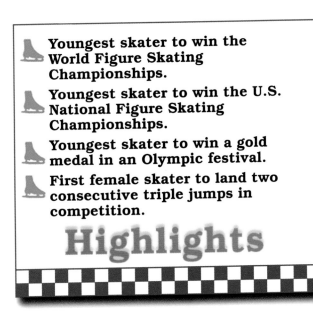

- Youngest skater to win the World Figure Skating Championships.
- Youngest skater to win the U.S. National Figure Skating Championships.
- Youngest skater to win a gold medal in an Olympic festival.
- First female skater to land two consecutive triple jumps in competition.

## Highlights

Tara is always working to become better. Skating fans know her best for her jumping ability. Before her triple-**loop** combination, she also mastered the difficult triple **salchow**-triple loop combination. Despite the difficulty of her skating programs, she maintains an artistic flair. She works with **choreographer** Sandra Bezic to make her skating programs as beautiful as they are athletic.

Tara's skating takes a lot of time out of her day, but she loves every minute of it. A typical day has Tara getting up around 7:30 a.m. and hitting the ice by 9:00 a.m. She skates until around 1:45 p.m., then takes an hour lunch break. Her favorite foods are spaghetti and other pastas, as well as chicken and steak.

In addition to at least five hours of skating practice a day, Tara studies at home with tutors. They work with her on math, science, social studies, reading, and Spanish.

# Inspiring Other Kids

Tara loves spending time with other young people. She makes a special effort to visit young people most in need of cheer.

During the 1996 holiday season, Tara participated in an exhibition in Los Angeles. While there, she visited The City of Hope National Medical Center. The center is known around the world for its work in treating people suffering from cancer, diabetes, HIV/AIDS and other serious illnesses.

Tara's visit was a highlight for the young patients at The City of Hope. Likewise, Tara enjoyed it.

"I just enjoy spending time with these kids," she said. "I know how fortunate I have been with my opportunities, and if I can share some of that with others or help them in some way, then that makes me happy with what I'm doing."

Tara also took time out during the U.S. Figure Skating Championships in Nashville, Tennessee, to visit children at Vanderbilt Children's Hospital.

"Since it was around Valentine's Day, I brought little Valentines to give to the kids," she said. "I have fun doing these hospital visits. It makes me feel good to know that I helped brighten up someone else's day, and I think the kids in the hospital like it, too. Sometimes it's a smile or a hug, or just simply their mom saying 'thanks.'"

**Tara Lipinski finishes a performance at the 1997 World Championship.**

# Cool Under Pressure

The top female skaters in the nation had gathered in Nashville, Tennessee, in February, 1997 for the 78th Annual U.S. Figure Skating Championships. For Tara, the competition was fierce, including defending champion Michelle Kwan, 16.

Tara performed her short program, also known as the **technical program**, perfectly. She was the last skater to perform her long program, or **free skating program,** the final night of the competition. Tara was in second place as she prepared to take the ice. She knew she could win the championship with a perfect performance.

"I just wanted to skate two great programs," she said of the competition. "My goal was to make the world team."

As always, the cameras were rolling, but that didn't bother Tara. "You know everyone's watching you, and you just have to go out there and show them what you can do," she said. Tara no longer even notices the cameras.

Tara always has been cool under pressure. That night was no exception. She skated another perfect program, including her amazing triple jumps. No judge gave her a score lower than a 5.8 out of 6. The gold medal was hers, along with a trip to the World Figure Skating Championships.

The skating world quickly took notice of this tiny wonder—only 54 inches (137 cm) tall. People began to compare her to other famous skaters. They mentioned names like Peggy Fleming, Dorothy Hamill, and Kristi Yamaguchi. All of those women were great U.S. ice skating champions. Yet none of them earned a national title at age 14.

**Opposite page:
Tara Lipinski takes
another award.**

21

# On To New York

Even though Tara works very hard, she does take a break now and then. She likes to shop. New York City is Tara's favorite place to go shopping. She had a chance to do that and more after winning the U.S. Figure Skating Championship.

While in New York, Tara was a guest on the Late Show with David Letterman. "I was so excited," she recalled. "What was I going to say? What was I going to wear? Everyone was so nice—they made me feel like it was no big deal, just go out there and have fun. So, I did." Tara said she felt very short compared to the tall David Letterman!

Tara also appeared on the Rosie O'Donnell Show. "She was so funny," Tara said. "I couldn't stop laughing. I never knew she was such a big skating fan. She knew all the names of the jumps and all about past skaters. I had a blast just meeting her before the show."

Rosie also gave Tara a very special present—a picture of Tom Cruise!

**Left to right; Gusmeroli, Lipinski, Kwan at the 1997 World Championship.**

# Youngest World Champion

Even after all that fun in New York, Tara couldn't wait to get back on the ice. Following her gold medal win at the Championship Series Final in Canada, Tara went to Lausanne, Switzerland. The World Championships competition was going to take place there.

Once again, Tara turned in what was becoming her trademark—two perfect performances. She also made history as the world's youngest Senior Level skater.

The World Championships was an exciting time for Tara. "The short program felt great," she said. "I gave it all I had, but I was really nervous. I always get nervous before competition, but this was the World Championships. So, I went out there and tried not to think of it as the biggest competition of the year, but as doing any other program in practice."

"Then came the long program. That day, I tried to act as if it were just another day. I went to a little restaurant and had some pizza, and then went back to my hotel and just vegged out," she added. "I skated late that afternoon, and really, the hardest part was after I skated—waiting! Once I stepped out onto the ice, I felt better. With each jump I landed, I gained more confidence. By the end of the program, I knew I had skated my best, and I was so happy with myself."

The judges agreed Tara had skated her best. She won the gold medal. She also became the youngest skater in the history of competition to win the world championships. She was one month younger than famed Norwegian skater Sonja Henie was when she won her first world championship in 1927.

The win came as a surprise to young Tara. "I think I was in shock for about a week," she recalled. "I couldn't believe that I had won."

**Tara at the World
Championships in 1997.**

26

# Looking Toward The Olympics

Tara used to dream of going to the Olympics in the year 2002. Now she has her eyes on the 1998 Olympics. Yet the road to an Olympic gold medal will be long and hard. She will have to defeat fellow U.S. teammate Michelle Kwan.

"They're both great champions," said Tara's coach, Richard Callaghan, of the two skaters. "It depends on who's better on a particular day."

Skating fans know Tara for her turning and jumping abilities. Fans know Michelle for her artistic flair. The two may well be competing against each other for many years to come. After three Olympics from her first World Championships, Tara will still be only 23 years old.

In fact, the International Skating Union had to make an exception for Tara. The Union recently set an age limit for skaters to participate in international competitions. They set it at 15 years. Since Tara competed in the World Championships in 1996, the Union allowed her to compete again even though she was only 14.

No one knows how long Tara will be making headlines in the ice skating world. "She knows she can check out any time she wants," said her mother, Patricia. "We know anything could happen—an injury, a growth spurt or maybe she just doesn't want to skate anymore."

"Ask her what would happen if it all ended tomorrow," her mother added. "Know what she says? 'I'd start doing something else.' "

Knowing Tara Lipinski, whatever that is, she would do it well. That's the mark of an awesome athlete.

**Opposite page: Tara Lipinski works very hard at her sport.**

# Glossary

**Audition** - A trial performance to test a person's skills.

**Choreographer** - A person who plans and arranges the movements, steps, and patterns in a performance.

**Free Skating Program** - Usually a four minute performance set to music of the skater's choice.

**Loop** - A jump that takes off from the back outside edge of a skate and lands on the same edge.

**Lutz** - A jump that takes off from the back outside edge of the skate and lands on the back outside edge of the other foot.

**Salchow** - A jump that takes off from a back inside edge of a skate and lands on the back outside edge of the other foot.

**Technical Program** - A two-minute-and-forty-second performance set to music of the skater's choice. The program must include eight required elements.

**Triple Loop** - A loop with three twists in the air.

# Index

**B**

Bezic, Sandra  13
Bloomfield Hills,
   Michigan  8
Blue Sword competition
   9
Bobek, Nicole  8, 12

**C**

Callaghan, Richard
   8, 27
Champions International
   Skating Series  11
City of Hope
   National Medical
   Center, The  17
Cruise, Tom 11, 23

**D**

Detroit Skating Club  8
double loop  5

**E**

Edmonton, Alberta  10
Eldredge, Todd  8

**F**

Fleming, Peggy  21
free skating program  19

**H**

Hamill, Dorothy  21

Henie, Sonja  26

**I**

International Skating
   Union  28

**K**

Kwan, Michelle  19, 27

**L**

Lausanne, Switzerland
   24
Letterman, David  22
Lipinski, Jack  6, 8
Lipinski, Patricia  6, 28
Los Angeles  17

**N**

Nations Cup  15

**O**

Olympics  27
Ontario, Canada  11

**P**

Paris, France  11

**S**

Slutskaya, Irina 12

Skate Canada  11
Sugarland, Texas  6

**T**

technical program  19
triple flip  5
triple loop  5, 13
triple lutz  5
triple salchow  13
Trophy Lalique  11

**U**

U.S. National Junior
   Figure Skating
   Championship  10
U.S. Olympic Festival  9
U.S. Postal Service
   Challenge  12
United States Figure
   Skating Association  9

**V**

Vanderbilt  18

**W**

World Figure Skating
   Championship  10, 20
World Junior Figure
   Skating Champion-
   ships  10

**Y**

Yamaguchi, Kristi 21